MW01106654

IT'S MY LIFE!

DIZZY ANGGUN

PARTRIDGE

Library of Congress Control Number:		2021920117
ISBN:	Hardcover	978-1-4828-7901-8
	Softcover	978-1-4828-7899-8
	eBook	978-1-4828-7900-1

To order additional copies of this book, contact
Toll Free +65 3165 7531 (Singapore)
Toll Free +60 3 3099 4412 (Malaysia)
orders.singapore@partridgepublishing.com

www.partridgepublishing.com/singapore

CONTENTS

This book is a memoir. It reflects the author's present recollections of experiences during her childhood journey.

Some names and characteristics have been changed, some events have been compressed, and some dialogue has been recreated.

Keep away from people who belittle your ambitions.
Small people always do that, but the really great ones
make you feel that you too can become great.

—Mark Twain

PREFACE

It looks like I am taking a longer time to complete this book than I expected since I started it in 2009. I realise there are many more memories that I want to share. I started writing my journey when I received a mini laptop that I dreamt of as a birthday present in January 2009. I knew instantly that this is my working partner to share with friends and others about my life as a naughty child.

I dedicate this book specially to my son. Though I have not shared much about my childhood life with him, he seems to take it after me in many ways. Coincidence? I call it the work of God.

Life is beautiful—what more can I ask for?

A journey down the memory lane began.

MY ARRIVAL

I was born at home in 1966 in a small village located in the eastern side of Singapore. The only thing that would remind anyone of this village now is the mosque still standing opposite the new buildings of shopping malls and offices.

According to the midwife, I came out together with the sac still intact. I would have suffocated or died, she told my mum. However, according to the Chinese belief, a child born in a sac could actually see ghosts, so they thought; and the child is also known to be stubborn. Many would agree that I am definitely a stubborn person. I have been an active child since I was a baby. I was always "on the move," crawling my way around. I fell off the wooden bench at the verandah many times when I crawled around on my own. I survived the falls without any scars—amazing!

My dad was hoping for a baby boy after my eldest sister, but a girl appeared in this world instead. Since Dad was so certain that it would be a boy, the clothes waiting for me were for boys. I ended up wearing boys clothes for a while. Probably, that is why I behave like a boy.

GETTING TO KNOW BOYS

I started to know the boys at a very tender age of five. I played marbles with my male cousins and neighbours. Growing up, I have never owned a baby doll. The boys in my life treated me like one of them. I climbed trees, played in the drains, fought and behaved like a boy.

MY STYLE

My mum liked to dress us siblings in matching clothes, and I hated that. One day I deliberately fell onto a puddle of water and managed to change into my favourite dress. I already know what "sexy" means at that age too. I begged my mum to sew a sexy long dress for me. "Make sure the back is open wide 'til my butt!"

On the first day of my primary school in 1973, I must have been the sexiest seven-year-old girl in school. To think that many people thought I was trying to attract men with my sexy clothes just because I have bigger boobs now.

I was always wearing shorts and never liked to be seen in a skirt unless it was the school pinafore. Another of my favourite fashion style is "the shorter, the better." Once, in 1976, a man in the bus stared at me. It was my light blue shorts that he was staring at. "What is your problem?"

If those eyes could kill, that guy would have died instantly. In fact, until recently, I still like wearing shorts and feel comfortable in them. My son thinks that wearing long pants make me look shorter anyway.

Once I was called to the centre of the school assembly area in 1983. "Why is your PE (physical education) shorts so short?" the PE teacher asked in a stern manner.

"Teacher, please tell me why call it a short if it is not even short?" I replied in a sarcastic way.

I was lucky that I did not end up in the detention class.

Sexy and short clothes are not the only favourites. I love wearing my traditional clothes as well because they also make me feel sexy. When I put on the mini kebaya, I feel like the famous Malay actress, Salima—an epitome of a modern Malay woman. My aunt said I looked like my mum when I am in my kebaya because my mum liked wearing one. The Indian saree takes me to a life full of colours—happy and beautiful. The only traditional clothes that I have yet to put on is the Chinese cheongsam; I guess I have to lose more weight to fit into my pink cheongsam that has been hanging in my wardrobe for the longest time.

Lately work has made me appreciate another traditional attire—the dirndl. The women in Germany wear this traditional attire during their festive celebrations, especially during the Oktoberfest. I also own the lederhosen worn by the men. I look as good on the lederhosen—it makes me feel like a man. Luckily, I am no longer that skinny, gaunty girl anymore.

IT'S GOOD TO FALL SOMETIMES. YOU WILL LEARN TO GET UP AND PROBABLY LEARN NOT TO FALL AGAIN (OR MAKE THE SAME MISTAKE AGAIN).

MUM'S FASHION SENSE

Mum thought wearing a size bigger would make my shoes and clothes last longer. I ran around the school hall one day with my big shoes, and the shoes just flew off my feet. The teacher reprimanded my eldest sister because my shoes were always "flying" around the hall when we sang and danced during the music lessons. Another "long-lasting" clothes that I owned was my *baju kurung*—a traditional dress for Malay ladies. It was so loose that it could fill two chickens in it. In fact, I looked like a Chinese opera singer in a costume.

PRESCHOOL

I have never been to a preschool because my parents did not think I need that, or maybe we could not afford it back then. I learnt the alphabets from my eldest sister just days before school started. I was not able to sing "Twinkle, Twinkle, Little Stars" and "Baa Baa, Black Sheep" because these were the songs the children learnt in their preschool years. Sadly, until today, I am not able to sing those songs, neither to my son nor to my grandchildren!

CHILDHOOD REWARDS

In 1974, my primary two English teacher gave us cherry tomatoes when we did well in her class. I was good at spelling and managed to earn many tomatoes every day. I was greedy and not willing to share my "earnings" so I kept them in my pocket, only to find them crushed by the time I got home. One day Ms Jane rewarded me with a large guava from her garden. I decided to eat it quickly. Suddenly, something popped out from my mouth. It was my tooth.

ALL THE MONEY YOU HAVE ARE NOT YOURS ALONE. SHARE THEM WITH THE NEEDY TO ALLOW MORE TO COME.

SCHOOL EXAMINATION

I never believed in school revision—I would be playing at the school field when others were busy revising for the examination. The amazing part was I was still first in class. Somehow that concept no longer works for our children now. Now I definitely hope my son will not follow my "lazy" footsteps.

At this age, I have to study for all the courses that I attended—no excuse—but at least the brain is still functioning well because I passed all the six papers that I took in 2010. I passed another exam in 2020 after the second attempt, not too bad because many had to take more than three times.

OLD WET MARKET

I helped my mum buy groceries and do marketing—fighting my way at this wet market with the aunties and uncles, negotiating for good buys. I was good at that even at the age of ten—I was a negotiator long before Kevin Spacey became one (in the movie *The Negotiator*). I was always more willing to go to the market because I had a crush on the guy who sold the grated coconut. He obviously did not even notice me because I was only ten, and he was probably already eighteen.

Fast forward to June 2011—now as I visited this market with my husband, I realised that it is no longer the same. The stalls are more organised, and the signs are modern. Luckily, the ambience feels the same for both of us as we enjoy going to the market. However, my husband is obviously a better cook. Hence, he decides on the things we should buy, and I just follow behind him. Standing in one corner while he goes around buying stuff has caused some stares from the people there because it is normally the wives that would be fussing around the market while the husbands wait. He simply enjoys cooking with fresh ingredients.

THE PERSON WHO IRRITATES YOU JUST NEED THE ATTENTION, GIVE IT TO HIM OR WALK AWAY.

MY SIBLINGS, MY LOVE

1975 - My youngest sister has an acquaintance living in the same apartment as ours. However, this girl, Chee, always teased and made fun of my sister. I had to ensure that she understood that no one messes with my family. One day, as she walked by, I approached her and showed her just that.

It also reminded me of a man who came knocking at the window screen of my car in 2005. The man looked fierce and arrogant. He was upset that my nephew was close with his daughter and said that it was making his wife very sad. I told him, "Why don't you tell your wife to stop crying and discipline your daughter instead? A girl should be able to take care of herself and not simply blame the boy."

He walked away—I guess he underestimated me. Nobody messes with my family.

Once I was against my eldest sister going out with a guy because I did not trust him. Every time he came by to visit, I will stare at him and refused to greet him. True enough, he was not serious with her.

WHEN YOU REACHED THE TOP, YOU MUST REMEMBER THE JOURNEY UP, OR YOU WILL FALL HARD.

MY MOTHER

I remember my mum as a generous lady who loved to cook for people. For someone who has never gone to school, she learnt how to cook very well from her aunt when she was young. Unfortunately, that is the trait I failed to acquire from her.

All her siblings, nephews, and nieces loved her presence—they knew that delicious meals would be on the table each time my mum came visiting. She baked very well too—my eldest sister and I were selling *kuehs* (Malay cakes) that my mum baked. Her *apam Malaysia* was so good that it literally cured this sick neighbour after eating it.

My form teacher in primary five (1977) did not like me because I was never nice to her. She told Mum that I might fail in the coming exams. My mum was devastated and cried. What an inconsiderate teacher she was. Of course, I did well that year.

The same teacher told the class that "basketball is a rough game" during one of our physical education lessons. That was definitely an opportunity to me—I pushed her and hit the ball at her. "Why did you push me?" she shouted angrily at me.

"Well, it is a rough game as you mentioned earlier, right?"

That hit was deliberate—for hurting my mum's feelings. These people just have to know that nobody messes with my family, especially my mum.

NEVER WAIT 'TIL TOMORROW TO TELL SOMEONE THAT YOU LOVE HIM, IN CASE TOMORROW NEVER COMES!

MY TEACHERS

We were supposed to wear new traditional costume for the Malay dance performance (1980), but the second language teacher, Cikgu Ahmad, gave it to the girls from the upper secondary as he favoured them. One day he came by to my class and requested me to help him carry his books to his car. "Can you please help me carry the books to my car?" When we reached the carpark, he said, "See the scratch on my car? I know who did this."

"Good, if you know, sir. Maybe next time you'll keep your promise," I replied.

My form teacher reprimanded me in front of the class, and as the class monitress, I felt insulted (1981). My good friend Cheng and I removed the nuts from the wheels of my form teacher's car. She did not turn up at school the next day. She came back to school the next day, told us that her car has a malfunction.

Another second language teacher, Cikgu Ali, teased me with my classmate, Zed (1981). I was so embarrassed and humiliated at the same time. I took a rubber band and snapped it directly at him. The teacher requested for an apology, but I refused. Since then, I had a hard time in his class.

Once I argued with my maths teacher, Mr Beng. He is a nice man, but I probably was not behaving myself anyway. As stubborn as I am, I let him know that if anyone puts their hands on me, I will not allow it.

My favourite teacher would be Cikgu Ismad. Even though he teased me lots in class, I think he did a great job teaching us the language. Once he told me, "Even though you look so fierce and rough, you are a very sensitive girl." True.

THE NAUGHTY ONE?

The Indian stallholder at the canteen of my primary school once told mum, "Your eldest daughter is so well behaved, but this one . . ." He sighed, pointed at me. "She opened all the covers of the candy bottles and ran away without buying any."

Nevertheless, when I visited him once after I left the school, he remembered me straightaway and thought that I was actually nice (just playful).

However, a classmate, Han, wrote in my autograph book on the final year at school (1984). She wrote this on my page: "The Most Sarcastic Girl in School!" When I asked her why she did that, she said, "I want your other friends to know about you."

I wondered why she did that, but I tore that page in front of her—I don't need such negativity and reminder of this person in my life. Nobody can take away the way I am (except God)—no one should ever be me.

One day, "You know what?" a girl was asking her friend as they walked down the escalator. I was behind them, listening to their loud conversation. "Do you know?" she asked again.

Her friend did not answer her, so I did. "I know," I said with a cheeky smile.

"Huh? What do you know?" She turned around to look at me.

"I know what you know," and I walked away, leaving them with their mouths wide open.

NEVER UNDERESTIMATE A WOMAN'S STRENGTH—MENTAL AND PHYSICAL. IT'S STRONGER THAN ANY MAN'S PHYSICAL STRENGTH!

BOYS ARE NAUGHTIER!

A family friend was flirting with me one day at my cousin's home. I got so mad when he tried to tickle me, and I let him know I will not allow it. He complained to my mum. Her reply was plain simple: "You asked for it!"

My mum knew me very well. She might not approve of the many things that I did in life, but I know she would understand why I did it.

I went to the Ken Fried Chicken located in the east one day when I was in secondary one (1979) with some classmates for a banana split. There was this guy working there whom I was interested in when I was twelve. He came up to our table and said sarcastically, "Wow! I didn't know you can afford this!"

I was angry at his comment—I guess he was upset that I initiated the "breakup." I got mad and started to fill the empty bowl with iced water to the brim 'til it spilt to the floor. When the supervisor came by, I told him, "Your staff is rude, make sure he cleans this mess!"

My classmates almost fainted when they heard me. I paid for the banana split and left the restaurant.

I made my classmate Zach cry once or maybe twice or maybe too many times. He always found a way to bully me, and each time I reminded him I will never allow it. We are still friends till today. Surprisingly, he likes me after those many incidents. I was glad that I was in a coeducation school because I had the opportunity to fight with the boys.

Another classmate, Eng Kee, was always first in the subject History, and I was second. He was always so proud of his achievement and made faces at me for not being able to outdo him. One day my British classmate, Ivan, helped me get bed bugs from his home, and I put these creatures on Eng Kee's chair. It was definitely a joy watching him scratching his thighs with all the red rashes.

We were at St Anthony's Island (1979) as part of our camp outing. This classmate, Fahrin, took the meat from the BBQ pit, tasted it, and asked me, "Why is the meat so sandy?"

"Oh, it's just the spices," I replied.

I deliberately gave him the meat that has fallen into the charcoal pit because he was always making fun of me in class. I think that he is a mean boy.

"Is your father Godzilla?" I teased this boy, Fandi, in school (1983).

His last name sounded like the dinosaur. He was known to be a gangster in the institution where I was studying, and many boys were so afraid of him. He was fuming when he heard me. "I'm going to punch you!"

"Okay, meet me at the gate after school," I challenged him.

He did not even turn up at the gate. The next day I saw "Godzilla" at the corridor. "What happened, no balls?" I provoked him.

He turned and charged at me and hit me against the metal cabinet. I fell to the ground and went after him to give him a nice big punch.

IF YOU DON'T HAVE PASSION, LIFE LOSES ITS SHINE!

BOYS—AGAIN

We went to the beach after our curriculum activities on Saturday (1981). A Frisbee hit my leg, and it hurt me bad. This regular army guy, Kaleb, had to chase and beg me to return it to him while I continued walking. "Look at where you're throwing next time!" I blasted at him.

We later became close like siblings because his mother missed his sister who was travelling so much as a musician. He is still with the army—true Singaporean.

I went out for a root beer with this army guy, Trinity (Kaleb's friend), to the defunct root beer restaurant. His camp mate was there too with his girlfriend. When asked who I was, Trinity told him that I was his girlfriend. I got angry and put my slippers on the table. I only put them down on the floor when he confessed to his friend that he was lying. I made him walk home with me from the beach in the east to where I lived (about 5km) just because he said that he was not used to walking. He mentioned that he only took taxis to ferry him around. I hate men who are show-offs.

BOYS? NOT AGAIN!

I was introduced to this senior in my secondary school, Sabar. He was a good writer and play director, but he was so protective. He wanted me to listen to him. Me? No way I'll do that! Since then we never talk anymore, even though we ended up acting together in the National Drama Competition in 1982. I was nominated best supporting actress that year. One of the directors in those days, Mr Len Ali, thought I was a natural in acting. Update: Sabar passed away recently in 2021, deepest condolences to his family.

I cried when this schoolmate, Nazar, thought that even though I am cute, I am not feminine enough for him. I was very upset, but another schoolmate, Edward, reminded me that in life, we can never please everyone. He said I should look at it as part of life. That was painful, even though it was the truth, that I was never feminine in school.

I enjoyed teasing this schoolmate, Wayne. We always ended up on the same bus, bus service 21, every evening to go home (1980). I called him names and even asked others to stay away from him. He was cool about it, and I must say I lost the battle that I created. There was actually attraction.

In fact, instead of hating me, he came to my class to give me a small book to read—how romantic can that be? I had the book with me until 2007, when my son tore it up accidentally. We were two different human beings: He was quiet, and I was (am) talkative. He is rich, and I am not. And the best part is he never hurt my feelings, but I always hurt his. However, I was sad to make the decision to stay away from him because I knew the relationship might not work because of the differences, and I do not want to hurt him more.

In March 2009, Wayne told me that he remembers me as being *manja* (loves to be pampered), sensitive, *manis* (sweet), and enigmatic. He did not even think that I was naughty. He admired me because I always know what I wanted. Amazing! Until today, he seems to be the *only* one friend that knows me so well. I cannot believe that his observations of me during schooldays were remarkable.

There is one thing I learnt from my mum:

> ***Be generous, help people whenever you can. Your life will not be blessed if you are greedy.***

I love you, Imuk! (That's what I fondly called her.)

A MAN IS A GREAT LEADER ONLY WHEN HE HAS A GOOD ADVISER—HIS SOULMATE!

MY SECOND COUSIN, FIRST BOY IN MY LIFE

I saw a boy and a girl kissing at the field while on the way to the shop. I was nine years old then. They looked like they enjoyed it. It must be nice. Anyway, at eight, I already know how to feel for the opposite sex—I was attracted to my second cousin who used to represent the country in Singapore Football League.

We played marbles together with the rest of the boys when we were growing up. I never had a doll to play with and no girl friends back then, living in the kampong. My cousin and I had so much fun together. We even had the opportunity to go on a helicopter ride.

Then we went to schools nearby—I was in the girls-only school, and he was at the boys'; both schools were located near Jalan Tembus. We had the same destination after school—behind the dental clinic where my mum and his grandmother (my mum's eldest sister) would be waiting for us.

By that time, we no longer talk. We sat close to each other but never uttered a word. It is like we suddenly became strangers. Not a word. We did not even look at each other. Well, that's life.

MY FIRST CHILDHOOD BOYFRIEND

I had my first boyfriend when I was twelve (1978). He was not even interested in me, but I was convinced that he would fall for me one day. Eventually, I succeeded. He was already working, and I was taking the PSLE that year. Remember the guy who worked at Ken Fried Chicken? Yes, that was the boy. I was in love. I forgot about the exams. Mum cried so much—she was worried for me. What if I fail in the exams? Mum's tears brought me back to reality. I have to try to do well. I told him that we were over. How can I fail because of a man? He should not take me away from responsibility—my responsibility. I was fortunate I still had time to revise.

I went back to the books—dated with the books every night. It paid off. I passed and went to the school of my choice—my first choice. About 90 per cent of the girls went on to the all-girls secondary school, and I decided to be in the mixed school. For the first time, I was exposed to boys and finally became one of the boys. In our recent reunion, we met again after twenty-seven years, and I was still one of the boys—in fact, I was the only lady there. I felt like I am back to my schooldays again at that moment.

FOOLISH ACT

I was contemplating whether to confess in this book about something that I am trying to tell my son not to even try it. I was in the morning session in 1976, while my youngest sister was in the afternoon. Hence, I had to return to school in the afternoons to fetch her. One day I met another schoolmate who was also waiting for her sister. While waiting for our sisters, we realised that we were getting bored. She then took me to the freezer at the canteen, which was already closed by that time. She showed me the fridge that was filled with the packet milk, where the students had ordered earlier for the day. The packets in the fridge were the remaining ones from the daily stock. She said these packets would be thrown away anyway and suggested that we should just take and drink it. I was hesitant about taking them because I knew it was not a right thing to do, but at the same time, I was also craving for the milk as I could not afford to purchase it. The girl convinced me that we would not be caught; after all, she has done it many times before. She said I might as well drink it since I was there. I took the banana milk and definitely enjoyed it.

Once there was an incident when I took a packet of sweets at the grocery store near home without paying and got caught.

The lady wanted to call the police, and I was shivering with fear, not about the police but thinking of the consequences if my mum would find out. I begged the lady to give me a chance, and because she knew me well since young, she let me go. That moment I felt her words were like a wake-up call. She felt that I was a good child. If someone believed in me, I should not disappoint her and, worst, disappoint myself.

I realised it was a mistake and stopped meeting the girl at school altogether. When she asked me to join her to the canteen, I told her that I was not thirsty and wanted to read. I did not think she would understand that taking things that do not belong to you is considered stealing. I decided to stay away from her; this was one friend I could live without. From that day onwards, I stopped drinking banana milk.

I was lucky that I realised this soon because there was a person I knew who was caught stealing a pair of jeans at the department store, and the police was called in. I was very sad. He was poor and wanted the chance of wearing a nice pair of jeans—the feeling of denim on his skin, feeling like a grown-up man. He was fortunate that he was not expelled. It would be bad because he was good in his studies.

IF YOU NEED A GOOD LEADER OR BOSS AT WORK, TAKE A LOOK AT HIS WIFE. SHE CONFIRMS HIS LEADERSHIP QUALITY.

MY HOBBY—DANCE

1976 - I imagined that I was a ballerina one night. I lost control and fell into the drain. My nose and face were bleeding badly. I had to hide behind my eldest sister to avoid Mum's scolding, but of course, she got the worse scolding for not taking care of me the moment Mum saw the blood on my face. Probably, it was not fair for her to take the blame, but we were young then.

Until today, I enjoyed dancing, and if alcohol can make a person tipsy or drunk, I am already "floating" in my own world when I dance. I would rather dance alone than dance with someone who simply do not know how to enjoy dancing.

Once in 2009, I was dancing alone on the upper floor of the Hard Café in Bangkok and singing to "Joanna" by Eddie Grand, sung by the lead singer of the live band there. The singer saw me, and I was called down to the stage to dance along with him. It was a great feeling to be on stage, especially when he chose me instead of calling this lady who was dancing alone in front of him, trying to attract his attention.

I AM LEARNING FROM LIFE, BUT WHAT IS LIFE? BELIEVE IN YOURSELF—LIFE IS A JOURNEY.

LOOKS ARE DECEIVING

This guy, Ras, (1988) spiked my drink during the staff party when I was working at the Shang Singapore. I kept falling off the chair after that and wondered why, and I was told that I was drunk. The next day I went to the staff cafeteria, looking for him. When I saw him, I grabbed a chair and hit him hard. "Next time, you are dead!"

My ex-husband also thought that alcohol is a norm in my life until I cursed him for bringing a mug of beer to me. The way people make a common judgement just by looking at the way you dress and talk. Until today, my former boss went to the extent of getting an alcohol-free beer to tempt me. All my life, I have never tried it, so I wonder what made him think that I would actually do it. Hard to believe that I was organising a huge event involving lots of alcohol yet never tasted any at all!

REMEMBER TO PAMPER YOUR HUSBAND ONCE IN A WHILE. HE IS MORE A KID THAN THE KIDS!

THE HEARTBREAKER, THE MATCHMAKER

Heartbreak no. 1

Boys—hmmm, nice. Good-looking ones too. I was attracted to some, and some were attracted to me too. I went to a movie with a group of boys. Smart move—it was a horror movie. I hugged the boy next to me. Smart move for him, but I was really not into horror movies because I am scared of ghosts, ghouls, etc.

We became good friends after that—he did not mind that I was the dominating one, and he was the obedient one. I actually did not like that, even though I occasionally enjoyed that he did what I requested him to do. Actually, he was not the first that I matched-make. When I learnt that this guy was still interested in me even after we left secondary school, I decided to meet him to find out why. He thought I was cute and lovable—like I have not heard that before. I asked him why he was still attracted to me despite being bullied by me in school. He even carried weights to build his muscles just to please me when I told him that he was scrawny in school.

To him, I was being myself and definitely a brat, yet he liked me for what I am. I thought that was crazy. Then I remembered there was a girl who was attracted to him when he was fifteen whom he met in one of the school camps.

He told me that when the girl told him of her feelings towards him, he showed her his girlfriend's photo—*me*. I scolded him for being so foolish to ignore her feelings for him. She was definitely a much better person compared to me—she was soft-spoken and patient. He deserved a good girl like that.

Yet he was still single when we met that year. He was still hoping to be with me—silly guy. I persuaded him to call her, and I actually gave him her number. (I kept his small yellow phonebook, which he had thrown away back then in school.) Every time I called him to check if he called her, he said he only wanted to be with me. Finally, I told him that he should move on and be with someone who wanted to be with him.

He reluctantly gave up on me and started to meet her.

Even though he was sure of his love for me, the relationship blossomed, and he finally married her—one good deed by me.

Heartbreak no. 2

I remembered breaking a man's heart—again. I was nineteen, and he was thirty. Love blossoms in situations that you least expect it. He was the guy who drove me and my other colleagues to work daily. He owns this small transportation business. Everyone who has been taking his transport for many years told me that he is a very serious man. They rarely see him smile. Well, one thing's for sure: He was not a good-looking guy, but I like his piercing eyes—they seem to penetrate into your soul.

As naughty as ever, I thought I should try to see his reaction with my silly ideas. I started to attract his attention by hitting the seats, the window grills, the metal poles with my pen just to irritate him. I could see that he was not pleased. He stared hard at me from the rearview mirror, but I continued despite being warned by the other ladies not to upset him.

As usual, the transport will drop me off at a school nearby for my night class. One evening, as I was alighting from the transport, I asked him if he was upset with my misbehaviour. He looked at me, and I waited for his answer anxiously. It seemed it was my turn to stare at him. Suddenly, he smiled, and I thought he actually has a nice smile. He was not mad at me all.

So I continued to tease him in front of the others. "Isn't that a handsome smile? You should smile more often."

He blushed, and the rest laughed. From that day onwards, he became more relaxed and could even chat with some of us on the transport.

One night after the class, I was walking towards the bus stop and saw the transport. I wondered why it was parked there at that time of the night. I approached it and was surprised to see him inside. I asked him what he was doing there and if he was waiting for someone. He affirmed it that he was waiting for someone—me. He asked me to get on the vehicle so that he could send me home. As we talked on the way home, I realised that he was actually attracted to me. I thought that was insane, especially after how I behaved. He thought that despite my mischief, there is one thing nice about me—loveable. I could not believe my ears because I have always been known to be this naughty girl that not many could tolerate. Of course, he was serious to be with me. He brought me home to see his parents and brothers. His brothers were all excited, hoping that they will finally have a sister-in-law.

They thought I was cute and beautiful—it was like *Beauty and the Beast*. Yes, I know I was mean, but at least he was a nice "beast." I was very happy with all the attention that I was getting from him, his family, and his friends.

However, I know that I could not be a wife at that age. I was just not ready for marriage. He was ready to marry me because of his age, ready to start a family. He was really in love with me.

I told him that I am a difficult person; I could bully him to do many things. To him, I am such an adorable sweetheart that he was willing to do anything, everything, to make me happy.

But I was not prepared to carry this huge responsibility that requires full commitment.

One afternoon I sat down with him in a quiet place and asked him if he was serious to make me his wife. He nodded and looked at me with fondness. I could feel his love, I could even hear his heartbeat. I knew I should not hurt this wonderful man's feelings. His feelings towards me were sincere.

I finally requested him to get married if he truly loves me—but to someone else. He was angry and wanted to walk away. I pulled him back and reminded him of his promise to do "anything, everything" for me.

I told him that he deserves better. I could see that he was really hurt, I could see tears in his eyes. The days went by, and I saw his sad face every day. He refused to talk to me anymore. The ladies pushed me to cheer him up because they noticed that he was easily agitated.

I decided to change my seat so that he did not have to see me from the rear-view mirror, and that was when I found out there was this lady who recently broke up with her boyfriend of many years. She was devastated. An idea came into my mind—maybe I could connect her to him, even though I thought she did not seem to be the kind that would attract him.

One day I deliberately asked him to drop me off last. I talked to him about her, and he was mad that I had the audacity to match him with her whom he thought was arrogant. I told him that at least she was ready for marriage because she was almost thirty years old herself. After much persuasion, he relented but agreed that I could write a letter on his behalf to ask her out.

Anyway, they met, courted, and got married! He stopped looking at me, and I decided not to take the transport anymore because somehow she could feel his heart was still with me.

Was I cruel? I don't think so—I was helping a man to lead a better life. Was I hurt to see him finally married? A little, I guess, but this was one drama of my life that I was proud of—I helped someone find a life partner. Hopefully, they are soulmates by now. Love can come later, I believe in that, yet I did not even try to give him and myself a chance to fall in love. Maybe it was for the best.

I met him recently, and I could see how his eyes sparkled the moment our eyes met. He still has feelings for me, but I, unfortunately, do not have it at all. I was just being a friend.

Heartbreak no. 3

When I was working at a business centre in a five-star hotel, I had an admirer who was one of the regular guests of the hotel. Whenever he stepped into the business centre, he will call out my name like it was a natural thing to do. Somehow it was difficult for me to fall in love with someone who lives so far away—long-distance relationship is definitely not for me.

He was hoping that I might change my mind, but that never happened. One day I introduced him to a colleague who had just went through a breakup. They talked and talked that I felt left out. But I was happy for them. He now has someone to look forward to when he visits Singapore—someone who would have dinner with him, someone who would talk to him and listen to him. Their relationship blossomed, and I was just glad that I brought them together.

BOYS HAVE MORE FUN!

When I went to secondary school, I realised that boys are more fun than girls.

Once we went camping with the class to St Anthony's Island. I actually slept with the boys in one room, while the other girls were in another. Of course, the teachers in charge were not worried about me being with the boys—I was just like a boy myself. In those days, we never have funny ideas towards one another—we were plain innocent. The only challenge was I preferred the cold temperature, while the boys preferred otherwise, so Jeremy and I were switching on and off the air-conditioner in the room the whole night.

WHEN YOU START RUNNING, REMEMBER TO STOP FOR A WHILE. YOU MIGHT FORGET WHERE YOU ARE HEADING TO OR EVEN THE REASON WHY YOU RUN IN THE FIRST PLACE.

BAD COMPANY, GOOD LESSON

I went to the beach alone one day (1982). I sat down near a group of boys. We chatted, and then what was that? One of the boys was swallowing a bunch of pills. The next moment he was blabbering. I was a little concerned, but it was his choice to get intoxicated, and I was fine with it. It was definitely not mine.

One day I went to this guy's home where his family enjoyed liquor like it was coffee. I was invited to join them. I watched them laughing away and enjoying themselves. They seemed oblivious to their surroundings. I wanted to enjoy too, but that lifestyle was not my choice.

I always reminded myself that I wanted to be able to recognise my parents when I reach home, and I definitely wanted to recognise myself. It was not about disappointing my parents. It was more about being a disappointment to myself if I have gone towards that direction.

Once I went to a birthday party that was held at an army camp. I enjoyed myself and was dancing all night long. I simply love to dance. I enjoyed myself that night, even though I did not participate in the massive drinking session.

I looked at him. He was smiling at me. I smiled back, but he did not know who I was. I realised he was floating. I saw the bottle. I saw the straw. He was sniffing glue! He was not aware of the surrounding. I did not want to be him.

He said it was good to forget about his problems, but the problems were still there when he sobered up, and in addition to that, his brain deteriorated slowly after that.

I have been fortunate to experience life with these people. These people, in whatever state they were in, have taught me a valuable lesson: Never enter into a situation if you are unsure if you can come out clean!

ME, JINX?

Jinx no. 1

There was this boy in the athletics group who was always trying to harass me. One afternoon, there were only he and I at the Segelang Secondary School stadium—the rest have not arrived for the training. He took the opportunity to take advantage of me. He carried me from behind while I was doing my stretching. I screamed, but nobody heard me. Before he could go further, one of our friends arrived, and he put me down.

While he was doing his run, he skidded just when he walked past me. It looked like a normal fall, but his thigh was torn badly with the flesh showing and the skin slit open on his leg that you could see his bone. An ambulance was called, and as he looked at me, he told a friend that I had cursed him. This boy never learnt his lesson. He tried again, which I have forgotten what it was, and he had to pay for it again.

However, the final straw was when he tried for the third time, and that was definitely the last time. We were training at the Machie Reservoir, and at one quiet path, he pulled me to him, and just when he was about to touch me, a man jogged by and stared. After training, all of us decided to go for dinner, and while we were crossing the road, the boy came running towards me. Suddenly, I turned around, and I saw that he was almost knocked down by an oncoming vehicle.

He must have thought that I was a jinx. He decided to stay away from me after that last incident. That was also the last time I saw him because he left the group. Few years back, I met him at a meeting. He obviously did not recognise me. He would have run away if he knew who I was.

Jinx no. 2

One day, as I was walking along a stretch of road near an army camp, a motorbike slowed down, and I heard whistles from the rider and his pillion. I ignored them, but the next moment I turned around, and I saw the pillion was thrown off from the bike and hit the ground almost instantly. I was so shocked. I realised that another motorbike has hit them from behind when they were slowing down to tease me.

The two boys survived but not without open wounds with lots of blood. I did not do anything to hurt them, I just ignored them.

POTENTIAL TRENDSETTER

For some haters, I was an attention-seeker, but I would rather consider myself as a trendsetter. I was not doing it to get attention from others anyway. I just enjoy the style I chose to be in.

Days when school shoes had to be white, I went to school wearing a pair of black ones. I wanted the shoes for so long that when I finally managed to buy them, I decided to wear them to school even though they were black. Unfortunately, the school principal found out when she spotted the shoes on the shoe rack outside the music class. I was called out to explain, and I told her nonchalantly that my white school shoes were wet.

GENTLE REMINDER TO MYSELF – YOU WILL NOT BE POOR SIMPLY BY HELPING THOSE IN NEED!

PAIN IN SILENCE

I remember the day after my mum passed away, I was awakened by a rattan stroke that almost hit me, but I managed to stop it. I remembered the words that came out from that person. "Now that your mother is no longer around, don't try to be a spoilt brat anymore."

Suddenly, I felt so alone without my mother. She was the only one that understood me, and I guess I was the only one that understood what she was going through. I was considered her favourite, but I never got away with the beatings. She beat me anyway if I did wrong, and I was definitely a naughty child (in case nobody noticed that).

A couple of times, I tried to leave home, but I realised that no matter how bad the situation is, you can still count on your family, and I never want to be "lost" in the outside world. I have seen too many people who were influenced by the bad company and their lives became so messed up. I need my life, I love my life, and nobody is going to mess it up.

I gave in many times, even though it was not my fault. Many people judged me, said that I am arrogant, I always want to win, I always think that I am right, I have no respect for others, I am so judgemental, so on and on. Until today, they fail to realise that I do not deny nor affirm their judgements. Of course, I am angry and, most of the time, sad of these accusations because they actually do not know the truth—the real me. Whenever words said of me reached me, I choose to stay mum. No need confrontations because my conscience is clear. Today I was told that I hurt and offended a certain person, and I should apologise before it is too late. I tried to make peace, but it was not good enough. I have heard that people said that I am too strong to handle, but I am no robot. I have feelings too. People hurt my feelings, abused me with their unkind words, and even physically threatened and abused me. What did I do to them? I still talk to them. Call me stupid, but until today, I do feel traumatic over the past. When I occasionally spoke my mind, I hurt their feelings. One even called me a terrorist for wanting the truth because that was considered an "attack" from me—and that was all I did, being outspoken, being real.

I am now tired of giving in and pretending like those things never happened. So be it! I shall not retaliate, I shall not respond. They can continue to be in their own world, and I will mind my world myself. I was advised to be the first to apologise because "no harm done if you apologise." No harm done? Are you crazy? I have always been the first to apologise since I was a child, even if it was not my fault! Damn, I am done with all these. Nobody is going to take me for granted anymore. Behind that so-called strong character they think I am, I have always been the submissive one, the obedient one. The only difference from a typical obedient and submissive woman, I wish to be heard. I have a brain that I can think. I want to be able to share my points and even emphasise my thoughts. I never plan to rule the world because (I know) God knows that women will wreck the world if they head the world—women are one bunch of emotional creatures. For that, I sometimes wish I was born a boy.

BULLY

Do you know what I should call people who treated me badly in my life? BULLIES! While waiting for my son, I saw a girl bullying her schoolmates. She poured a glass of drink onto this boy's plate of rice. And the boy was still eating. At that moment, I thought about my days in school. I know I was naughty, but I have never treated a friend in that manner. I only rebutted if I was bullied, but I would never start first.

That poor boy actually continued eating his rice. If I was his age, I would have chased after her and punched her. However, that could be me thirty years ago talking, or is that anger still in me? I have to do a self-reflection.

Just the other day I was driving on lane 1 on the highway. When I saw a black Mazda speeding from behind, I moved to lane 2. Then a purple Honda Fit was driving slower than the speed limit and continued to stay on lane 1. Instead of overtaking the Honda, the Mazda actually followed behind closely. For more than 1 km, they both irritated each other, and then when the cars reached Chu Chu Kang, the Mazda overtook another Japanese-made car and slowed down in front of that car. What a sight! I did not slow down to watch the show, but what I learnt from this scenario is that we, Singaporeans, are bunch of stressful people—for the wrong reason.

I FOUND MYSELF—AGAIN!

Now I found my true self again after fifteen years. Hey, I'M BACK! Watch me roar! Easier said than done. There are days when I would cry for no reason; maybe there was a reason for the tears.

- I wonder if there is someone out there who will accept me the way I am.
- I do not want to be alone, I just want to be loved.

The good thing is I am happy and satisfied on most days—I am blessed with lots of opportunities and am able to cherish every moment of life. I am fortunate to be surrounded with good friends—not many but they are there for me.

YOU SHOULD LOVE UNCONDITIONALLY, SO THEY SAY, BUT IT SEEMS THAT THERE ARE SO MANY CONDITIONS TO FALLING IN LOVE!

LOVE CONQUERS ALL, DOES IT?

I realised love doesn't come easy for me; it is not easy to feel love. I met an old friend from another school whom I have been close with for many years—only through the phone. He has a long scar on his left arm, but I could not remember how he got that. We only talked on the phone, but one day, when his girlfriend left him, we decided to meet. I like him straightaway because he brought me the biggest Garfield plush toy I have ever seen. He even gave me another one for my birthday. We enjoyed talking for hours on the phone, and one day I joked with him, "Why don't you and I become a couple?"

I was surprised that he agreed. We started to talk about marriage, but we decided not to proceed because it was not meant to be.

After four years of "long distance" courtship and ten years of marriage, my first marriage went down. I thought I failed, but now I believe that maybe *we* failed. The partnership was for two. It is over now, but life has just begun when my son came into my life in June 2002.

As I held him in my arms, I asked myself, "Is he the one for me?"

It had to be. I actually prepared the baby stuff for him. I bought everything that a newborn should have at a children's store in town. The salesgirl was pleasantly surprised to entertain me.

A DREAM GIVES YOU HOPE, A HOPE GIVES YOU COURAGE, A COURAGE GIVES YOU STRENGTH, AND A STRENGTH GIVES YOU PERSEVERANCE.

MAGICAL MOMENTS

In January 2010, I told myself that I am ready to embark into a new stage of life. Actually, it is not a new stage but another chance to go through the path again. I want to be married again, but I was not about to force any man to marry me if one is not committed. There is no point to marry someone for the sake of marriage. I also do not want to be abused. So I waited.

I was recommended to get to know two men that should fit well with my criteria: a Muslim man who is able to guide me and to love me and my son. I was attracted to the first one, but it was not meant to be because he is still "searching" after fourteen years of being a single father. With his look and a nice smile, he definitely has many admirers. I was reluctant to reach out to the second man, even though I kept seeing his name. Finally, I decided to talk to him one late night. We talked and talked all through the night, and I enjoyed every minute of it.

After few days of talking to him on the phone, I decided to surprise him. I drove up to his area with my son; he thought I was just kidding. That's me—when I want something, I will go to the end of the world to acquire it. At least I did not have to do that to meet him. The pictures he sent me were deceiving. I like him better in person. In fact, when our eyes met for the first time, there was a strange connection. According to research, if you look into the other person's eyes for eight seconds straight, it means you have fallen in love at first sight! Wow!

That first meeting was great and interesting. We had lunch, we went to the beach, and we even met again in the evening for a movie. And because my son likes him instantly and wanted to see him again, seriously, it was my son that was attracted to him so much. I cannot deny that I was not. He did not wait long to propose because he cannot imagine losing me. Even though I am keen to embark on another journey again, I was a little concerned that his proposal came too soon. He is certain, and his decision is final—he wants to marry me. The reason: Only we both know why.

We got engaged, and for the first time in his life, he got to choose the ring he likes. It is a white gold ring with a big garnet stone surrounded by small diamonds from Tian Jewellery. Garnet is my birthstone. He even presented me with my favourite flowers—a bouquet of white tulips.

WHAT MAKES YOU THINK YOU ARE RIGHT JUST BECAUSE YOU THINK YOU ARE RIGHT?

MY HORROR-IBLE ... JOURNEY

I was told that if a child is born together with the sac, she or he will see ghosts easily. Jinx or sixth sense? I believe I am intuitive—used to be stronger when I was younger.

Mother woke me up before she passed away—I was sleeping, and suddenly, I heard, "Wake up, I am leaving now!"

His late wife came into my dream and apologised for the daughter's misbehaviour

Instinct told me that there will be something rolling down, and I would fall if I continue to cross over—it was a mineral water bottle that rolled down.

DON'T COMPETE,
JUST COMPLETE EACH OTHER.

RELIEF TEACHER

I was a relief teacher when I was seventeen years old. I taught literature to secondary one students. The amazing part was the teacher herself was impressed with the way I taught her students to appreciate poems and also how the poem was interpreted in the most artistic way. You go, girl!

STALKER

I was stalked by my student almost every day, and it did not help that we were staying in the same neighbourhood. I always ended up on the same bus with him, even though I tried to avoid that, because he would change bus just to be with me.

OTHER TALENTS GONE UNNOTICED

A.   I *designed* a dress with two chiffon layers, and months later, a socialite dressed in the same design was featured in *Singapore Tatler*. I did not know who the designer was for that dress.

B.   My *intuition* said, "If you go down the bus now, you will fall." I paused, and something really rolled down.

C.   When my mum was dying in the hospital, I knew that evening might be the day, and I decided to stay by her side. "Wake up now, I'm leaving!" I heard her in my sleep, and yes, she left us that morning, at 4:15 a.m.

D.   I chose Parisienne perfume by YSL just before it became the *it* perfume of the season. In short, I think I have an *eye* for what will sell.

MY THOUGHTS!

Words of wisdom by me, so I thought, created me and
not intended to insinuate anyone in particular.

If any of these words are related to any
source, they are purely coincidental.

You may not agree, you may not like it—I am fine with
that because no one needs to debate on these words.

I didn't see it.

I can't believe it.

But I feel it.

A lot of times you lose your "soul"
when your "mate" leaves.

Sometimes we contradict ourselves because in life,

it does not always go as planned.

Do not let go of something

that you cherish.

It may not come back to you again.

Making conclusion is not my strength;

At least my intuition is.

Be yourself.

You will eventually have to struggle to get out

from what others want you to be.

Being you is real.

If you cannot trust yourself to commit,

Never blame others if they fail you.

I am definitely moving

But never moving on.

(I must have written this during my sad days.)

Do you have to trust to love?

When love blossoms, you just have to know it and accept it

because trust is so fragile that

you might even break it without
knowing it and will not accept it.

Disappointment is when you form an expectation

That you yourself cannot achieve.

They say a way to a man's heart is through his stomach,

but to me, what's important is his mind.

There is only one thing in a man's mind!

Get that right!

You can no longer be yourself when

you enter into marriage.

A part of you will be lost along the way

to adapt to the needs of your other half.

I have to learn not to love too much.

I have to learn not to care too much.

I simply cannot handle the hurt too much.

Every one of us lies.

We just have different reasons for it!

Paper qualification does not guarantee
that you are intelligent.

It merely confirms that you can take instructions well
and you have good memory to memorise what you learn.

If you do good,

Don't tell.

If you have done bad,

Don't blame others.

It is difficult to cope with life

when you are alone.

It is worse if you have someone

in your life that makes it difficult.

It is better to be alone!

First, you must develop your heart.

Why?

You need it to feel before doing anything else.

Do you know that there is nobody who is stupid?

So why even have that word in the dictionary?

It's for that man who likes to think that

he is more superior and others

are plain stupid.

I don't need to have more wrinkles—

from people who already created

their own wrinkles!

It's all in the mind.

But I am not going to allow anyone to control it.

I'll take care of it myself!

If your thinking starts to get

Erratic,

Everything starts to get

Chaotic.

The truth and being true can be hurting,

BUT

they are REAL.

I am not perfect.

But I perfect it by ignoring you.

If you are not smart, don't be evil.

Evil will lead to self-destruction.

I AM . . .

I AM IN LOVE WITH MY SON.

He gives me strength and the will to
continue life with courage.

I AM MYSELF WHEN I AM ALONE.

Looks like the real me is never acceptable with people around me. I am supposed to take a different persona when I am with them.

In most cases, I am what I am!

I AM TRAUMATISED BY ABUSE.

Physical and verbal abuse can kill—my soul.

Obviously, my weakness is not being able
to fight the trauma . . . 'til today.

I AM INTERESTED IN LIFE.

The biographies of many people inspire me.

I AM INTERESTED IN PEOPLE

People make me tick.

It does not matter if they are nice or not.

Either way, there is always a lesson to be learnt.

I AM NOT ALWAYS NICE.

I simply do not see why I should always be nice.

I can try to smile more instead.

I AM NOT YOUR TYPICAL KIND OF AUNTY.

My mind and body never feel the age that I should be.

Feeling young makes me accept that life is wonderful

despite the challenges we face every day.

I AM PESSIMISTIC.

That is definitely my downfall!

However, on a positive note, it makes sure
that I do not take life for granted.

I AM WILD.

I realise if I listen to a hardcore and grunge music, I can be so motivated to turn wild, and if I am driving, I could just accelerate to the fullest and speed.

It makes me see the positive side of life better!

I AM FUNNY—SOMETIMES.

My jokes are spontaneous and most times can be dry,
so I do not think I could even write anything funny here.
I am just glad that I could still make many
people smile with my silly jokes.

I AM . . . STRONGER THAN A MAN.

Once my car drifted into a small drain—only the front tyres were in it. Thinking that I would not be able to get it out, I called a friend for help. He decided to reverse the car so that the tyres could be pulled out. I decided to go in front of the car and lifted it until the tyres could move when he engaged on the reverse gear.

PEOPLE SAY I AM . . . ARROGANT.

Maybe I am—if you meet me for the first time. I do not believe to be this sweet girlish lady who wants attention from people. Why not? Nobody tells me that I should pretend to be nice!

PEOPLE SAY I AM . . . BOYISH

Some boys treated me as one of them because I was not ladylike. I was always with the boys because girls are too petty.

PEOPLE SAY I AM . . . A GANGSTER

Definitely I was and still am!

1. I hit a boy with a broom when he tried to touch me.
2. I punched the Canadian guy who dared me, and broke his jaw.
3. I challenged a boy in school for a fight after making fun of his name.
4. I told off one father to see me if he has a problem with my nephew.
5. Someone just told my husband that I was such a gangster that my boss is afraid of me (I wonder where he got that idea from?).
6. Scenario @Event: "Are you waiting for him?" asking to the woman who was so bold to sit next to the band leader for my event. "Yes," she answered. "Are you planning to go to his room?" I questioned her and she answered, "That depends." "He is coming with me and so are the rest of the band, so I guess you should just leave." She was fuming mad, got up and demanded an apology from the leader. "Why should he apologise to you?" She just walked out.

Last but not least, I would like to share this story from the first workshop I attended back in 1986. This inspirational talk was given by Mr Andrew Sng, and the story that I understand goes like this:

There was this priest who died and has gone up to queue up to be in heaven. He saw the long queue and thought he should look around for anyone that he might know. Suddenly, he saw his neighbour also queueing up to go to heaven, and he is ahead of him. The priest was really unhappy about this; he was wondering how this neighbour could end up in heaven. He saw Saint Peter walking by and stopped him. "Can you please tell me why my neighbour is also going to heaven?" he asked Saint Peter.

"What is the problem? You are also going to heaven, right?" Saint Peter replied.

"But you do not know him. He was a gambler, a womaniser, a drunk. He should go to hell!"

Saint Peter tried to pacify him that it should not matter much as the important thing is both are going to heaven, but the priest was not satisfied still. Therefore, Saint Peter decided to take him to another room to show him how his neighbour was able to go to heaven too. "Let's watch this TV monitor and see what happened when you both were still alive," Saint Peter said.

The first scene showed the priest preaching in the church; the monitor moved to show the congregation attending his service. There was this lady buffering her nails, a boy reading a book, these two people busy talking and laughing, and one even fell asleep. "But take a look at what your neighbour did," Saint Peter mentioned.

The next scene showed the neighbour as the bus driver, a little drunk, was about to start his engine, cursing and swearing as he did that. The passengers straightaway started to pray for their lives. "So now you know why he is going to heaven, right? He made people pray despite his bad behaviour," Saint Peter commented.

The way I look at it, life is amazing, and things happen in the most twisted and unique way that we should not take it for granted and not judge people as what they seem to be. Thank you, Mr Sng, for sharing, which I have never failed to share with people around me until today.

A little introduction on Mr Andrew Sng, which I found from the web: Andrew Sng is the senior partner (Asia) of Decision Processes International (DPI), an international management-consulting firm that specialises in helping organisations transform their business practices through critical-thinking processes.

Thanks to my wonderful mum for allowing me to be myself and not trying to change me. She is the best, and may Allah SWT bless her soul. Amin.

Thanks to Dad too. I was never close to him because he hated my guts, but deep down, I know he loved me anyway.

Yes, I loved him too. We just cannot see eye to eye. May Allah SWT bless his soul. Amin.

Thank you, God, for giving me this life—I have been blessed. Please continue to give me the strength to face the rest of it.

Finally, thank you to my good friends, JK, Wad and RJ for believing in me and inspiring me to write this memoir. I could not do it without your encouragement and support. Everything happens for a reason—it is a matter of whether the reason is good enough for us.

I now embark on a new journey with my new family, and I look forward to a more colourful life with them to keep me going, and may Allah bless all of us. Amin.

In life, I realise I should not give up. I should just let go and move on.

Certain things or people cannot change; hence, I have to change my way, i.e., stay away and continue with my journey.

CPSIA information can be obtained
at www.ICGtesting.com
Printed in the USA
LVHW090356201021
700928LV00001B/31